EARLY AMERICAN HISTORY

Slavery in America

By Bert Wilberforce

Published in 2024 by Cavendish Square Publishing, LLC
2544 Clinton Street Buffalo, NY 14224

Website: cavendishsq.com

Library of Congress Cataloging-in-Publication Data

Names: Wilberforce, Bert, author.
Title: Slavery in America / Bert Wilberforce.
Description: Buffalo, New York : Cavendish Square Publishing, [2024] | Series: The inside guide : early American history | Includes bibliographical references and index.
Identifiers: LCCN 2022053024 (print) | LCCN 2022053025 (ebook) | ISBN 9781502667786 (library binding) | ISBN 9781502667779 (paperback) | ISBN 9781502667793 (ebook)
Subjects: LCSH: Slavery–United States–History–17th century–Juvenile literature. | Slavery–United States–History–18th century–Juvenile literature. | African Americans–History–To 1863–Juvenile literature. | United States–History–Colonial period, ca. 1600-1775–Juvenile literature. | United States–History–Revolution, 1775-1783–Juvenile literature.
Classification: LCC E446 .W65 2024 (print) | LCC E446 (ebook) | DDC 306.3/620973–dc23/eng/20221104
LC record available at https://lccn.loc.gov/2022053024
LC ebook record available at https://lccn.loc.gov/2022053025

Editor: Therese Shea
Designer: Deanna Paternostro

The photographs in this book are used by permission and through the courtesy of: Cover, pp. 9, 20, 23 Everett Collection/Shutterstock.com; p. 4 Kingppin/Shutterstock.com; p. 6 Brookes slave ship, British Library/Wikimedia Commons; p. 8 Juan Garrido Azcatitlan/Wikimedia Commons; p. 10 1670 virginia tobacco slaves./Wikimedia Commons; p. 12 Charges and net proceed of 118 new Negroe slaves Charleston South Carolina/Wikimedia Commons; p. 13 A slave auction in Virginia/The New York Public Library; p. 14 $100 bounty for runaway slave, Richards' Ferry, VA (cropped)/Wikimedia Commons; p. 15 Scourged back by McPherson & Oliver, 1863, retouched/Wikimedia Commons; p. 16 Illustrations of the American anti-slavery almanac for 1840 (cropped)/Wikimedia Commons; p. 18 Timothy H. O'Sullivan (American - Slaves, J. J. Smith's Plantation, South Carolina - Google Art Project/Wikimedia Commons; p. 19 Oney Judge Runaway Ad (cropped)/Wikimedia Commons; p. 21 Osman [graphic]/The Library Company of Philadelphia; p. 22 Eastman Johnson - A Ride for Liberty – The Fugitive Slaves - Google Art Project/Wikimedia Commons; p. 25 William L. Champney The Boston Massacre, March 5, 1770/Wikimedia Commons; p. 26 Rainer Lesniewski/Shutterstock.com; p. 27 a katz/Shutterstock.com; p. 27 (inset) FreedmenVotingInNewOrleans1867/Wikimedia Commons; p. 29 (left) Slavepatrols/Wikimedia Commons; p. 29 (right) Family of African American slaves on Smith's Plantation Beaufort South Carolina/Wikimedia Commons.

Printed in the United States of America

CONTENTS

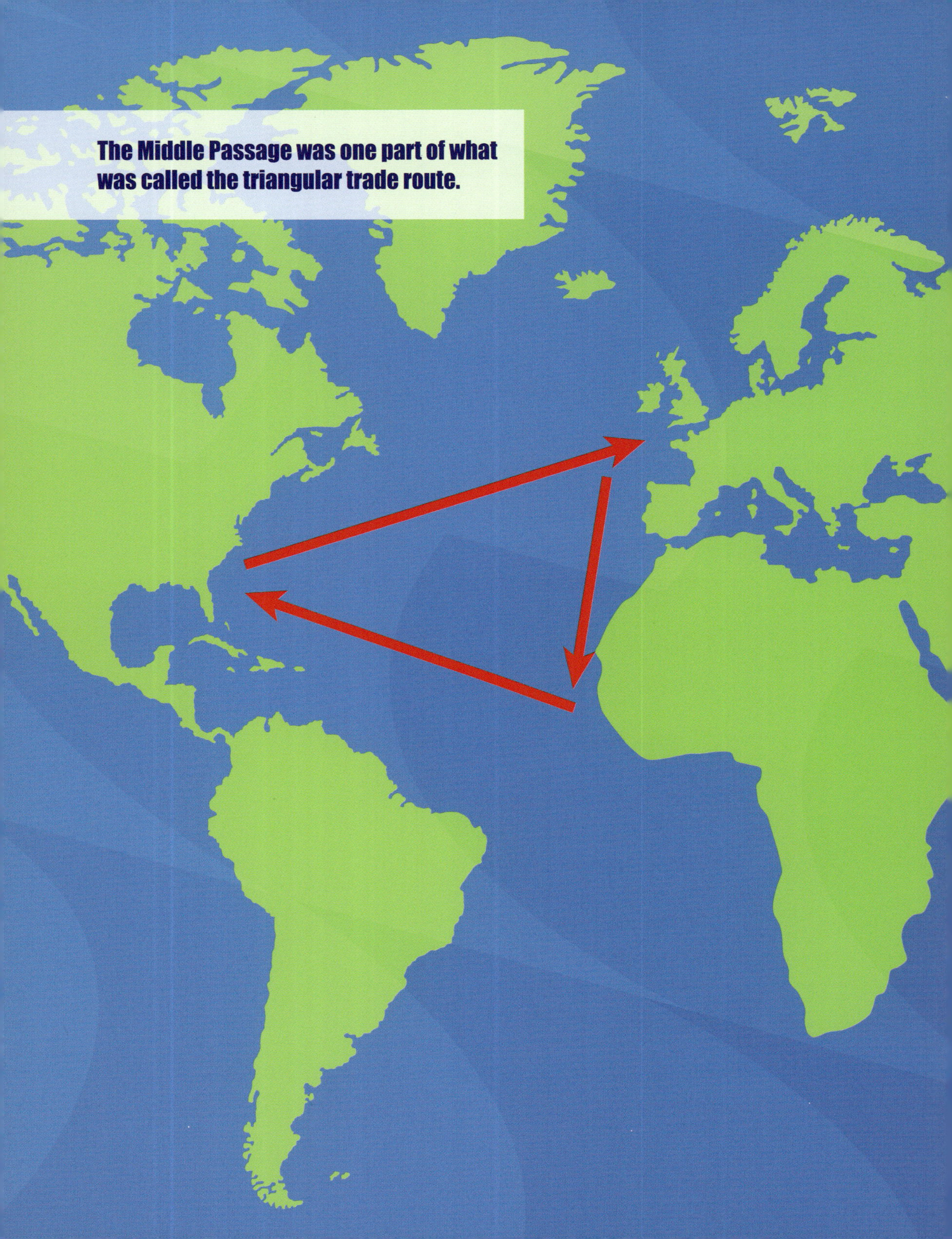

The Middle Passage was one part of what was called the triangular trade route.

JOURNEY FROM AFRICA

The story of slavery in early colonial America begins across the Atlantic Ocean. For years, the Dutch, Spanish, and Portuguese had been enslaving Africans and transporting them to Europe. They also took enslaved people to their colonies in North and South America. The British and French would later take part in this trade as well.

The long route to the Americas was known as the Middle Passage because it was the middle part of a three-part journey. First, Europeans went to Africa with goods and traded for enslaved people. Next, they took the enslaved people to the Americas in exchange for crops and other materials. Finally, they returned to Europe with those goods.

Fast Fact

Numbers about the African slave trade are estimates. Many records are wrong or have been lost over the years. Some enslavers bought and sold Africans secretly too.

Terrible Voyage

Life for enslaved Africans on the small, crowded ships was difficult at best and often deadly. They were chained together belowdecks with little room between them. Their only food was usually a little bit of rice, beans, or yams.

Enslaved people were permitted on deck for short periods of time. Sailors

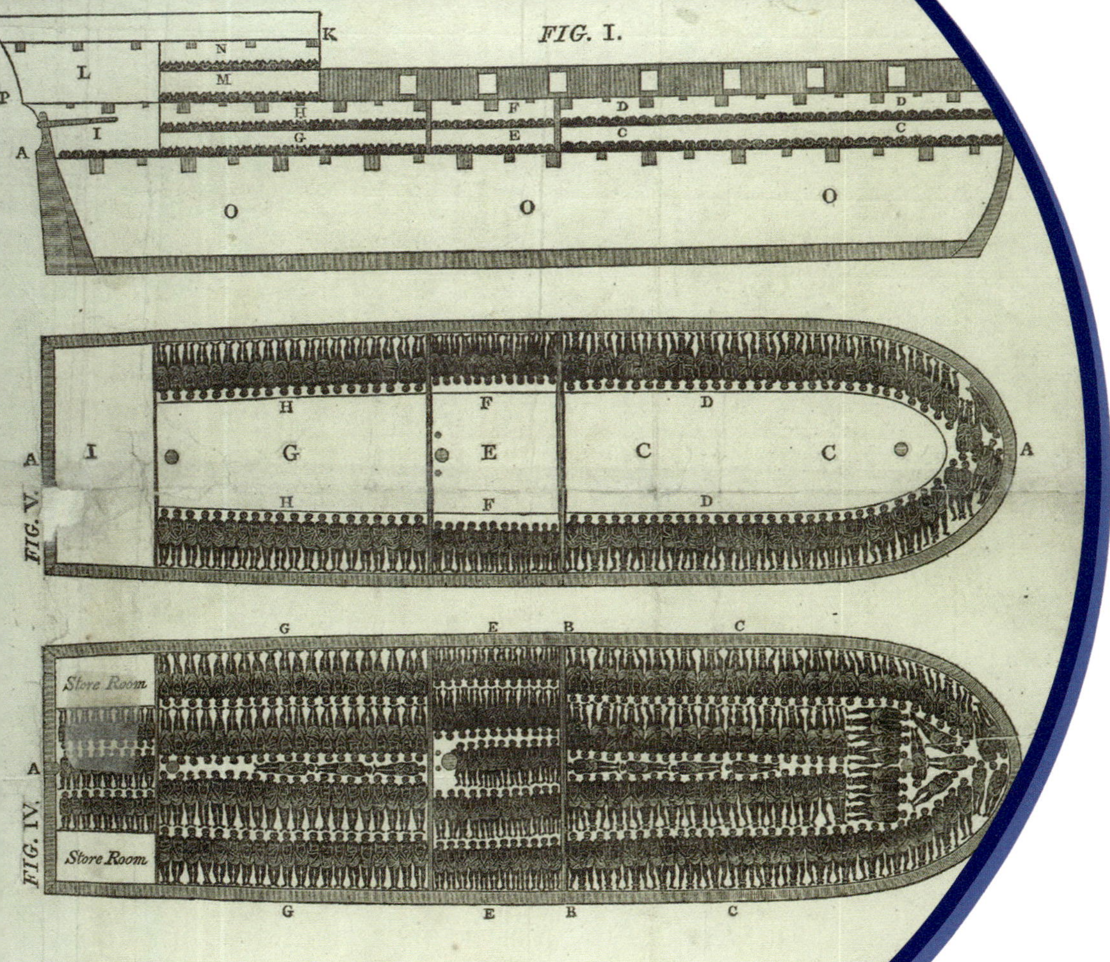

This diagram and description of a ship from 1787 shows how tightly packed Africans were during the Middle Passage. They were treated like cargo, not people.

forced them to sing and dance. Seas were often rough, and the voyage from Africa could take from weeks to months. Many Africans became ill on the journey, and many died because of the dangerous, or unsafe, conditions.

Between 1525 and 1866, these ships transported about 12.5 million Africans to the

THE LONG HISTORY OF SLAVERY

People have enslaved other people for thousands of years. Groups of African people often conquered and enslaved other groups. It was part of war. This was not much different from ancient Greek and Roman practices. When these people conquered new territory, they enslaved some of the conquered people. Slavery was also used to punish some crimes and as a way to pay back money owed. By the time Europeans were colonizing the Americas, royalty, church leaders, and farmers were enslaving Africans. The establishment of large farms in the colonies made the business of enslavement more profitable—and violent—than ever before.

Americas. About 10.7 million people survived the journey. Of those, about 388,000 were taken to North America.

Fast Fact

The enslaved people taken to Virginia in 1619 were likely from the Kingdom of Ndongo in west central Africa, today's Angola.

Taken to the Colonies

Historians think a British **privateer** ship (using a Dutch flag) brought the first Africans to the British colonies in 1619. About 20 to 30 Africans were traded for food at Point Comfort, near today's Hampton, Virginia. Governor George Yeardley bought seven of them. More arrived a few days later. Some of these Africans were enslaved. Others may have been **indentured servants**, with the hope of being free

A Black man, Juan Garrido, traveled with Juan Ponce de León in 1513 in his explorations through Florida.

some day. This event marked the beginning of the trade in enslaved people in the British American colonies.

These were not the first enslaved people in the North American colonies, though. In 1565, the Spanish brought enslaved Africans to a colony at what is now St. Augustine, Florida.

Slavery in Virginia

By 1619, Jamestown and other Virginia settlements were successfully growing tobacco and other crops. At first, British men **immigrated** to work in the fields. Colonial companies offered land to newcomers. However, the number of British workers could not meet the demand for laborers.

Virginia planters began buying more enslaved Africans. They paid with crops.

Fast Fact

John Rolfe—best known as the husband of Pocahontas—began growing tobacco in Jamestown in 1612.

By 1648, records show the number of enslaved people had jumped to about 300. By 1671, there were about 2,000. Traders were able to supply as many enslaved people as the colonists wanted, and the colonists continued to want more.

This 1901 illustration shows the ship *White Lion* bringing enslaved Africans to Virginia in 1619.

Many illustrations of early American colonies did not show the cruel and brutal parts of the enslaved life.

THE SPREAD OF ENSLAVEMENT

As more colonists arrived in North America, more settlements sprang up along the eastern coast. Fertile soil helped people establish more large farms. Traders in enslaved people brought thousands more Africans to the new colonies.

North to South

Some historians think Samuel Maverick was the first man to bring an enslaved person to New England when he arrived in the Massachusetts Bay Colony with two enslaved people in 1624. Around the same time, Dutch settlers in New Netherland used enslaved labor on farms. Maryland, too, relied on the trade in enslaved people after its founding in 1634, and enslaved Africans were recorded in New Hampshire by 1645.

Fast Fact

The colony of New Netherland came under British control in 1664. Parts of it became parts of six states, including New York.

The use of enslaved labor became a common practice in all the colonies. By 1700, there were nearly 28,000 enslaved people in the British colonies. By 1770, the number of enslaved people had grown

This is a record of enslaved people sold in South Carolina around 1754. They are marked on the document not by name but as man, woman, boy, or girl.

to 462,000. Most were in Virginia and Maryland, where they worked in tobacco fields. Many worked in rice fields in South Carolina and Georgia too.

Selling the Enslaved

Enslaved people were often sold at **auctions**. After an enslaver's ship docked, the Africans were forced off and gathered into a pen. They were washed and their skin oiled so they would look healthy. They were often branded with a hot iron so people would know they were enslaved if they escaped.

Then, each enslaved person was forced to stand on a raised platform

Fast Fact

Europeans enslaved Native Americans as early as Christopher Columbus's explorations. American colonists enslaved Native Americans as well.

THE CASE OF JOHN PUNCH

John Punch was an African indentured servant in Virginia. He ran away from the farm where he worked with two white indentured servants. All three were captured in Maryland and brought before a court in Virginia in 1640. All were sentenced to be whipped 30 times. In addition, the white servants were made to work four additional years. The judge sentenced John Punch to be enslaved for the rest of his life for running away, even though he, too, had been an indentured servant. This case shows how differently the law viewed those of African descent.

where buyers could view them. Buyers might make them turn around or check inside their mouth. They wanted the healthiest, strongest people possible.

Each enslaved person was sold to the highest bidder.

An enslaved family stands in front of bidders at an auction in South Carolina in this print from the 1800s.

$100 REWARD!

Ranaway from Richards' Ferry, Culpeper County, Va., 23rd instant, ABRAM, who is about 30 years old, 5 feet from 8 to 10 inches high, and weighs from 175 to 180. His complexion is dark, though not black, and hair long for a negro. He is a very shrewd fellow, and there is reason to believe he is attempting to get to a free State. I will give the above Reward if taken out of Virginia--$50 if taken 20 miles from home, or $20 if taken in the neighborhood. WM. T. J. RICHARDS,

Adm'r of Jas. Richards, Dec'd.

Sept. 24.

As early as 1643, colonies made laws that demanded that enslaved people who escaped be returned to their enslavers. Sometimes a reward was offered.

Families were torn apart. Parents and children were often separated forever. It was a frightening experience, especially as most newly enslaved people could not understand the languages spoken.

Slavery Laws

The early colonies did not have laws about enslavement. For many years, the differences between indentured servants and enslaved people were not clear. However, in 1641, Massachusetts passed the first law stating that selling, buying, and owning people was legal.

Fast Fact

In the 1600s, enslaved people in Virginia could take their owners to court over issues. The slave codes of 1705 made this impossible. Enslaved people became powerless under the law.

Virginia established slave codes, or laws, in 1705. They stated all enslaved people would be treated as property. Any servants who were not Christians in their native countries would be considered enslaved. The codes gave enslavers the right to punish enslaved people in whatever ways they wanted. They could even kill enslaved people and the law would support them. Other colonies soon made similar laws.

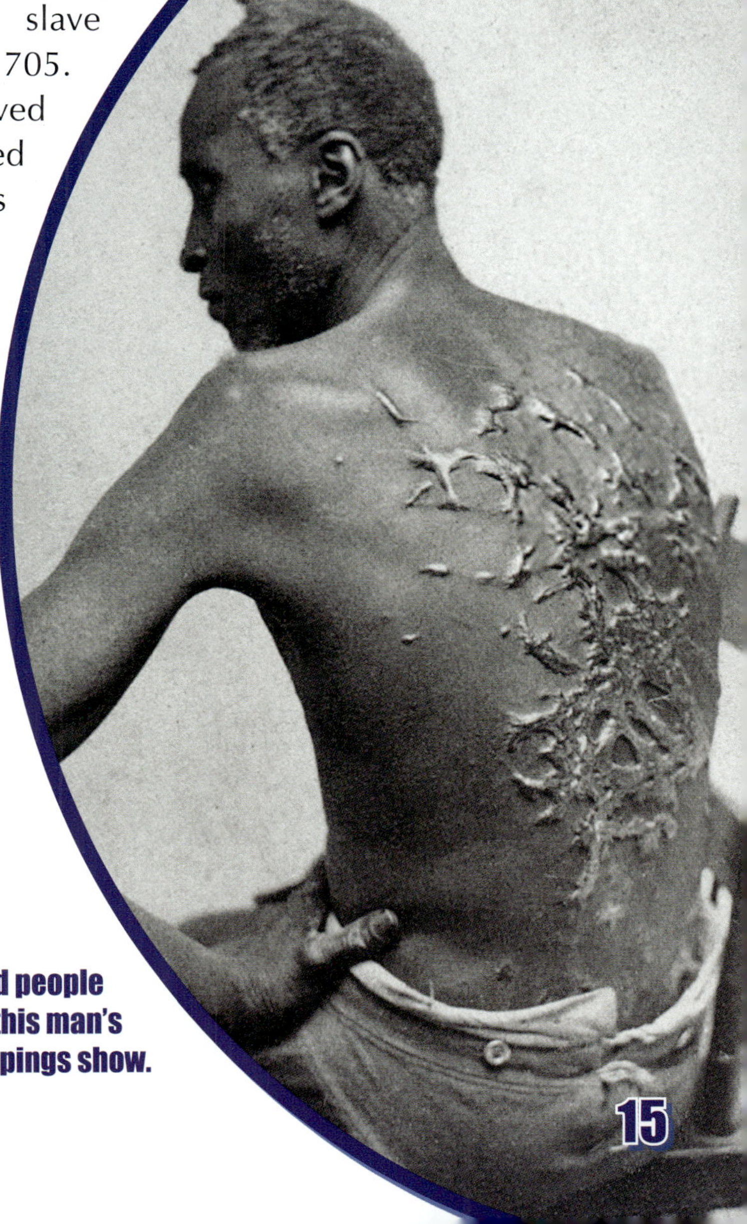

Punishments for enslaved people were often brutal, as this man's scars from whippings show.

Enslaved people who escaped were sometimes put in collars when they were caught and returned, as this 1840 illustration shows.

ENSLAVED LIVES

Enslaved people in the southern colonies mostly worked on large farms, sometimes called plantations. The southern agricultural economy depended on this workforce. The northern colonies' economies were more varied. Enslaved labor was used in northern businesses, households, and small farms. Some enslavers hired out their enslaved people so they could work for others. No matter the task, enslaved people were forced to work with little hope of a better life.

In the Field

Most of the enslaved people in the southern colonies worked in tobacco fields or on other kinds of large farms. They worked all year long, from dawn until after the sun went down, six or seven days a week. They tilled the soil, planted seeds, weeded the fields, and harvested crops. The enslaver or an **overseer** told them what to do—they did not choose their job. Often, they were only allowed to rest for a few minutes. Even ill or injured, they had to work.

Fast Fact

Some people were granted freedom from slavery after a time. Others managed to earn money and buy their freedom. However, most enslaved people did not have these options.

While rich farm owners lived in large, comfortable houses, their enslaved labor force lived in small cabins. Enslaved people are shown in front of their cabins in 1862 in South Carolina.

The amount of food, clothing, and shelter enslaved people received depended on their enslaver. Enslavers could sell them at any time, so families were broken apart without warning. Some treated enslaved people better than others, but many used harsh punishments such as whipping or starvation.

In the Home

Enslaved people who worked in homes or businesses—in both the countryside and the city—were called domestics or house servants. Most were women. They cooked, cleaned, made clothing, and took care of children. Men took care of horses and worked in gardens. Others were hired out to work in shops.

Enslaved house workers often labored seven days a week, whenever they were needed, even at night. Often, they had more to eat, better shelter, and warmer clothes than enslaved workers in the fields had. They sometimes were able to leave the house by themselves, most often to get food from the market. There, they could learn about current events or about their friends and family they were unable to see.

No. 43, ſouth Water ſtreet.

May 23 d1ot

Advertiſement.

ABSCONDED from the houſhold of the Preſident of the United States, ONEY JUDGE, a light mulatto girl, much freckled, with very black eyes and buſhy black hair, ſhe is of middle ſtature, ſlender, and delicately formed, about 20 years of age.

She has many changes of good clothes, of all ſorts, but they are not ſufficiently recollected to be deſcribed—As there was no ſuſpicion of her going off, nor no provocation to do ſo, it is not eaſy to conjecture whither ſhe has gone, or fully, what her deſign is;—but as ſhe may attempt to eſcape by water, all maſters of veſſels are cautioned againſt admitting her into them, although it is probable ſhe will attempt to paſs for a free woman, and has, it is ſaid, wherewithal to pay her paſſage.

Ten dollars will be paid to any perſon who will bring her home, if taken in the city, or on board any veſſel in the harbour;—and a reaſonable additional ſum if apprehended at, and brought from diſtance, and in proportion to the diſt

FREDERICK K

May 23

This ad describes an enslaved woman named Oney Judge who had run away. She worked in George Washington's house in Philadelphia, Pennsylvania, when he was U.S. president.

Fast Fact

Oney Judge ran away to New Hampshire, where she married and had a family. She was never freed.

PHILLIS WHEATLEY, POET

Born around 1753 in West Africa, Phillis Wheatley was captured and brought to Boston, Massachusetts, when she was about seven years old. John and Susannah Wheatley bought her to work in their house. Phillis quickly learned to speak and read English. The Wheatleys allowed her to study while working for them. In 1773, Phillis's book *Poems on Various Subjects, Religious and Moral* was published. She was the first Black person and first enslaved person in the United States to be published. John Wheatley freed her in 1773. Phillis later worked as a servant and died in poverty in 1784.

PHILLIS WHEATLEY, NEGRO SERVANT to Mr. JOHN WHEATLEY, of BOSTON.

Phillis Wheatley may have written about 145 poems in all, but many have been lost over the years.

Some enslaved people banded together to rise up against enslavers. Perhaps as many as 250 uprisings took place before the American Civil War (1861–1865).

A freedom seeker named Osman is pictured hiding in a swamp in this 1856 wood engraving.

Escape

Some enslaved people were able to escape into unsettled areas of wilderness, such as the Great Dismal Swamp in Virginia and North Carolina and the Bas de Fleuve area of Louisiana. They lived in small communities, raised crops and livestock, and stayed hidden. These people were sometimes called outliers.

Outlier communities existed through the Americas and grew until slavery ended. Many communities were established in the Caribbean and Brazil too. Most outliers lived peacefully, while some attacked farms and helped free others. Some were eventually recaptured, but others managed to remain free. A few communities grew so large and powerful that treaties were made with them.

This 1862 painting by Eastman Johnson, *A Ride for Liberty—The Fugitive Slaves*, shows an enslaved family escaping to their freedom.

TOWARD FREEDOM

Soon after the selling of enslaved people began in the American colonies, people calling themselves abolitionists began to speak against it. Members of Pennsylvania's Religious Society of Friends—Quakers—became some of the loudest early abolitionists. In 1688, several Quakers wrote the first North American document stating that slavery was wrong. Quaker Anthony Benezet founded a group that became the Pennsylvania

Anthony Benezet wrote against the practice of enslavement in 1748. Printed materials like this helped spread ideas about abolition and the evils of slavery.

OBSERVATIONS

On the Inflaving, importing and purchafing of

Negroes;

With fome Advice thereon, extracted from the Epiftle of the Yearly-Meeting of the People called QUAKERS, held at *London* in the Year 1748.

Anthony Benezet

When ye fpread forth your Hands, I will hide mine Eyes from you, yea when ye make many Prayers I will not hear; your Hands are full of Blood. Wafh ye, make you clean, put away the Evil of your Doings from before mine Eyes Ifai. 1, 15.

Is not this the Faft that I have chofen, to loofe the Bands of Wickednefs, to undo the heavy Burden, to let the Oppreffed go free, and that ye break every Yoke, Chap. 58, 7.

Second Edition.

GERMANTOWN:
Printed by CHRISTOPHER SOWER. 1760.

Fast Fact

George Washington owned enslaved people by age 11. In his will, he set the enslaved people on his land free, though not until after his wife's death.

Abolition Society in 1775. The abolitionist movement grew.

During the American Revolution

Enslaved people fought on both the British and American sides when the American colonies went to war with Britain in 1775. Some were forced to fight in place of their enslavers.

In 1775, Lord Dunmore, the governor of Virginia, declared that any enslaved people who fought with the British army would become free. Thousands escaped and joined the British army. American general George Washington later offered the same promise, a promise that was not always honored. The American Revolution ended in victory for the American colonies in 1783.

The Path to Civil War

Between 1777 and 1784, Vermont, Pennsylvania, Massachusetts, New Hampshire, Connecticut, and Rhode Island became the first states to free their enslaved populations.

Fast Fact

Some historians think about 20,000 Black men served in the British army during the American Revolution, while 5,000 to 8,000 served in the **Continental Army**.

When the U.S. Constitution, the highest law in the United States, was **ratified** in 1787, it permitted the enslavement of people. Then, in 1808, Congress banned the importing of enslaved people. However, because the children of enslaved people who were already in the United States still became

CRISPUS ATTUCKS

Crispus Attucks was the first person killed in the American Revolution. Historians think it is likely that he had escaped from a life of slavery to live in Boston. In 1770, American colonists threatened a group of British soldiers in Boston. The soldiers opened fire on the crowd, killing Attucks and several others. Some blamed the colonists for the violence, while others blamed the soldiers. No matter whose fault it was, the Boston **Massacre**—as it was later called—helped touch off the American Revolution. A statue honoring Crispus Attucks and four others stands in Boston today.

The death of Crispus Attucks is pictured at center in this image from the 1800s, based on an engraving by Paul Revere.

This map shows the division between the Union and the Confederacy (the southern states that seceded) in March 1862, during the Civil War.

enslaved, the enslaved population continued to grow. As the nation added new territory, questions arose about whether slavery would be allowed there. States made compromises, but these continually caused conflict. In 1861, the American Civil War erupted after some of the southern states **seceded** from the United States over the slavery issue.

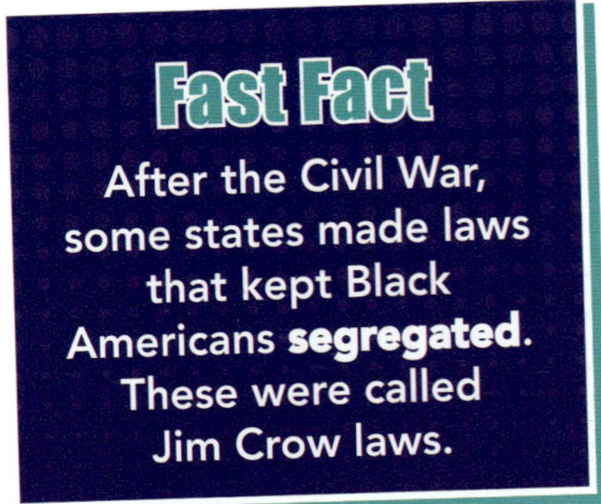

Fast Fact

After the Civil War, some states made laws that kept Black Americans **segregated**. These were called Jim Crow laws.

Abolition and Rights

After the Union victory in 1865, Congress passed three **amendments** to the Constitution. Ratified in December 1865, the 13th Amendment abolished slavery in the United States. In 1868, the

This illustration shows Black men voting in 1867 in New Orleans, Louisiana.

14th Amendment granted U.S. and state citizenship to anyone who was born or **naturalized** in the United States, including formerly enslaved people. In 1870, Congress passed the 15th Amendment, giving Black men the right to vote. Black women—and white women—got the right to vote with the passage of the 19th Amendment in 1920.

The end of the Civil War was followed by a period called Reconstruction. The goal was to reunite the nation, rebuild the South, and help the 4 million people who were freed from enslavement. However, segregation and **discrimination** against them continued for many years.

In 1964, Congress passed the Civil Rights Act, making it illegal to discriminate against people because of their race. The **descendants** of enslaved people were legally equal. However, the fight for true equality continues into the present day.

The Black Lives Matter movement began in the 2010s to bring attention to discrimination and violence against Black people.

A TIMELINE OF AMERICAN SLAVERY

1619 The first enslaved Africans arrive in the British colonies of North America.

1624 The first enslaved people are brought to New England.

1641 Massachusetts makes enslavement officially legal.

1688 Quakers in Pennsylvania condemn the enslavement of people.

1705 Virginia enacts slave codes.

1773 The Pennsylvania Abolition Society is formed.

1775 The American Revolution begins

1777 Vermont is the first state to abolish slavery.

1783 The American Revolution ends.

1787 The U.S. Constitution is ratified.

1808 Congress bans the importation of enslaved people.

1861 The Civil War begins as southern states secede.

1865 The Civil War ends. The 13th Amendment abolishes slavery.

1868 The 14th Amendment grants citizenship to Black Americans.

1870 The 15th Amendment gives Black men the right to vote.

1920 The 19th Amendment gives Black and white women the right to vote.

THINK ABOUT IT!

1. What challenges do you think free Black Americans and escaped enslaved people had in early America?
2. In what ways did enslavers try to make the people they enslaved seem less human?
3. Why do you think a separate amendment had to be made to give Black men the right to vote, even after they were granted U.S. citizenship?
4. Why do you think historians suggest using the term "enslaved person" instead of "slave"?

GLOSSARY

amendment: A change or addition to a constitution.

auction: A sale of goods where buyers bid against each other.

Continental Army: The army of colonists during the American Revolution, led by General George Washington.

descendant: Someone related to a person who lived in the past.

discrimination: Unfair treatment of a group, usually because of race, ethnicity, age, religion, or gender.

immigrate: To move to a new country.

indentured servant: One who signs a contract agreeing to work for a set period of time in exchange for money or other benefits.

massacre: The killing of a large number of people, especially when they cannot defend themselves.

naturalize: To grant citizenship to someone of foreign birth.

overseer: A boss or supervisor.

privateer: A ship that belongs to a person or company but is authorized by a government to engage in battle or to attack enemy merchant ships.

ratify: To give formal approval to something.

secede: To leave a country.

segregate: To keep people or groups separate from one another, often because of race or ethnic origins.

FIND OUT MORE

Books

Kawa, Katie. *Slavery Wasn't Only in the South: Exposing Myths about the Civil War.* New York, NY: Gareth Stevens Publishing, 2020

Lewis, Cicely. *Resistance to Slavery: From Escape to Everyday Rebellion.* Minneapolis, MN: Lerner Publications, 2022.

Smith, Elliott. *Jim Crow: Segregation and the Legacy of Slavery.* Minneapolis, MN: Lerner Publications, 2022.

Websites

American Anti-Slavery and Civil Rights Timeline
www.ushistory.org/more/timeline.htm
Read a detailed outline about the beginning of slavery to civil rights laws.

George Washington and Slavery: Key Events
www.mountvernon.org/george-washington/slavery/timeline-of-george-washington-and-slavery/
An outline highlights events in the lives of people enslaved at Mount Vernon as well as Washington's public and private actions concerning slavery.

Slavery—The Peculiar Institution
www.loc.gov/exhibits/african-american-odyssey/slavery-the-peculiar-institution.html
Learn about the history of slavery in colonial America and the early United States, including stories, timelines, and links to much more.

Publisher's note to educators and parents: Our editors have carefully reviewed these websites to ensure that they are suitable for students. Many websites change frequently, however, and we cannot guarantee that a site's future contents will continue to meet our high standards of quality and educational value. Be advised that students should be closely supervised whenever they access the internet.

INDEX